Sheep & the Shepherd

Roberta Ciucci

Art by Malinda Raines

Ciucci, Roberta
Sheep & the Shepherd
Copyright 2018 by Roberta Ciucci

Art: Malinda Raines
Editor: Kimberley Eley
Published by KWE Publishing LLC

ISBN (hardback) 978-1-7321034-2-9

All scripture quotations are from the New King James Version of the Bible.

KWE
PUBLISHING, LLC

For A. J.
Anthony Jermaine

Foreword

The 23rd Psalm was written by David, King of Israel. It is thought by many to be the most beautiful poem ever written. David's relationship with God was shaped by his understanding of the care a shepherd gives his flock, and he knew this so well because he had served as shepherd to his own father's sheep. What was well known to David, that sheep are defenseless and dependent, was universally understood at the time he wrote it but few of us today have first-hand knowledge of sheep. Because sheep have no means of defense, they are always nervous and fearful of attack by predators; the presence of a protective shepherd can meet their need and alleviate fear and worry. David lived one thousand years before Jesus yet he precisely described the role Jesus would fulfill as shepherd to mankind. Understanding this becomes a starting point on the journey toward understanding all of God's plan for us.

Acknowledgment

It is with deep appreciation that I acknowledge Dr. Mark Rutland who inspired me to write what would otherwise not have been possible. In his book, "21 Seconds To Change Your World," he patiently and thoroughly compares The Lord's Prayer and the 23rd Psalm and delves into the nature and habits of sheep, informing us about their temperament and behavior. Though I memorized the 23rd Psalm as a child, as many do, no one taught me anything about sheep to help explain it. Some of the lines were puzzling to me. I continued to enjoy the beauty of it but had what I now realize was an incomplete sense of its implied meaning. Now, thanks to Dr. Rutland's fine explanation, I have glimpsed the greater majesty of God's plan for sheep. I wrote this poem for young children with the goal of instilling in them the comfort that comes from understanding the 23rd Psalm as I do, and as an introduction to Jesus. My thanks are due Dr. Rutland for his enlightening contribution. May he continue to write and inspire his readers.

On the Sixth Day of Creation,

While the world was still brand new,

God formed his newest creatures and

They came in two by two.

He gave a special honor to
A very special few
In the family of woolly sheep
With ram and lamb and ewe.

They do not kick or scratch or bite
Or fight within the fold
For He fashioned them with innocence
Enfolding hearts of gold.

Sheep do not like fast-flowing waters
Found in stream and brook.
They fear the sound; they will not drink
Nor even come to look!

They need a placid pool or pond
With waters that are still
For then they sense it will be safe
To stay and drink their fill.

When sheep range far through meadowland,
They browse and graze all day.
To go and search for greener grass
They never know which way.

God saw the need and He decreed
A shepherd be their guide,
To watch by day and through long nights
And never leave their side.

His rod of iron keeps wolves at bay.
His staff saves lambs that fall.
He calls his sheep; they know his voice;
They follow one and all.

He leads his hot and thirsty sheep
Where cool, still waters wait.
They drink with ease and feel refreshed
As fears and cares abate.

Sheep hunger for fresh, tender grass;
He leads them to the best.
As he stands guard, it gives them peace
And they lie down to rest.

A shepherd cares for everything
A flock could ever need.
That's why it's said they shall not want
While shepherds have the lead.

God chose the sheep to show the world
How shepherds give them care:
They lead and guide, protect, provide,
With love beyond compare.

The message has clear meaning
For those who clearly hear:
God loves and longs to care for us,
To meet our needs and calm our fears,
To give us peace and wipe our tears,
To comfort and stay always near,
And hold us close as something dear,
Through all eternity's long years.

And so God sent his son to us,
A shepherd for our needs,
To be an ever-present help
In all our thoughts and deeds.

"I lay down my life for the sheep,"
Said Jesus long ago.
He came to be our shepherd
Because He loved us so.

Invite Him in to be your guide
To joy and hope and peace
And let Him fill your mind and heart
With blessings of hearts-ease.

John 10:15

He is The Bright and Morning Star,
The Prince of Peace, The Word,
And best of all, He told the world,
"I am The Good Shepherd."

John 10:15

DEFINITIONS

For words unfamiliar to children, these definitions may be used by the reader
when questions arise and a simple meaning is helpful.

Abate	To melt away - to decrease, diminish and come to an end
At bay	Kept at a safe distance by using a rod to fend off
Blessing	A gift of grace that brings happiness
Browse	To make one's way casually and randomly
Decree	An order by one in authority
Flock	A band of similar domestic animals herded together
Graze	To feed on growing grass while moving more or less on a course
Hearts-ease	Tranquility; peace of mind
Hearts of gold	Pure: without malice, without intent to harm
Honor	A distinction conferred with purpose
Innocence	Without capacity to injure
Placid	An undisturbed surface as smooth as glass
Rod	A long metal weapon of protection usually made of iron
Staff	A long wooden stick with curved crook on one end that extends a shepherd's reach to pull to safety a lamb that has fallen or strayed
Sheep Family	Ram: adult male sheep Ewe: adult female sheep Lamb: baby sheep up to 1 year old
Still waters	Waters without tide, current or flow
Want	To lack basic needs

Psalm 23

The Lord is my shepherd;
I shall not want.
He makes me to lie down in green pastures;
He leads me beside the still waters.
He restores my soul;
He leads me in the paths of righteousness
For His name's sake.

Yea, though I walk through the valley of the shadow of death,
I will fear no evil;
For You are with me;
Your rod and Your staff, they comfort me.

You prepare a table before me in the presence of my enemies;
You anoint my head with oil;
My cup runs over.
Surely goodness and mercy shall follow me
All the days of my life;
And I will dwell in the house of the Lord
Forever.

www.ingramcontent.com/pod-product-compliance
Lightning Source LLC
Chambersburg PA
CBHW042018090426
42811CB00015B/1675